REFLECTIONS
OF
A
WEEKEND
POET

outskirts
press

Reflections of a Weekend Poet
All Rights Reserved.
Copyright © 2021 Bill Smeltzer
v3.0

This is a work of fiction. The events and characters described herein are imaginary and are not intended to refer to specific places or living persons. The opinions expressed in this manuscript are solely the opinions of the author and do not represent the opinions or thoughts of the publisher. The author has represented and warranted full ownership and/ or legal right to publish all the materials in this book.

This book may not be reproduced, transmitted, or stored in whole or in part by any means, including graphic, electronic, or mechanical without the express written consent of the publisher except in the case of brief quotations embodied in critical articles and reviews.

Outskirts Press, Inc.
http://www.outskirtspress.com

ISBN: 978-1-9772-3602-9

Cover Photo © 2021 Nate Bollinger. All rights reserved - used with permission.

Outskirts Press and the "OP" logo are trademarks belonging to Outskirts Press, Inc.

PRINTED IN THE UNITED STATES OF AMERICA

Contents

The Forgotten

He shuffled down the sidewalk,
with a step no longer lively and light.
Not like before in another time,
when he went out to fight the fight.
Back then his step was light,
and careful with every stride.
He fought for and with his brothers,
the only thought was to survive.
Tonight he would sleep, wherever he could,
a park, or an alley, sometimes in the wood.
Homeless and forgotten, he no longer gave a damn,
he didn't care, and if he didn't, he knew no one else
would.
He would stare at an empty bottle,
like it was a crystal ball.
But he only saw past horrors,
the future didn't matter at all.
The things he had done, the things he had seen,
the many brothers who had fell.
He saw it all, a thousand yards away,
the blood, the pain, and the smell.
At war he had never felt more alive,
even knowing the night might not bring day.
But now he was empty and often wondered,
if he could keep the demons at bay.
He covered the scars on his body,
no way to cover the ones in his head.
He regretted his poor existence,

when so many of his brothers were dead.
So he shuffled along the best that he could,
and did his best day by day.
Haunted my memories and dreading the night,
and waited for angels to carry him away.

The Warrior

When he got out of school, he joined the Corps, did he know what he would be dying for?

Was it for the money, the fame or the fun, or to feel the weight of a death spitting gun. And a hawk was born and a hawk must die. The world creates them and then wonders why. In his heart he was a warrior and so he must fight, and as a warrior to die was his undetermined right. Alone in the hills and wounded as well, with the enemy closing and dealing with hell. He watched them charge and then he smiled, for when he died their blood flowed a mile.

They were coming in waves there must have been a hundred, he knew that he couldn't kill them all. But he said come on dying today's as good as any, I'll take as many of you till I fall. Blindly firing from the hip, curses flying from his lips, he takes a hit and turns a spin, on his face he wears a grin.

Shells ripping his clothes all around, slowly the warrior lets his knees touch the ground.

The enemy advances killing a lone man, but their blood flowed deep into the sand. And as a hawk lives, and as a hawk dies, the stillness is broken by a baby hawks cry.

The Christmas Truce

The war was in the fifth month.1914 was the year. Many would fight and many would die. There was was so much death and no cheer. The rain wet the ground and turned into mud, and the cold froze the mud solid. Conditions were poor and for the men, life in the trenches was squalid. On Christmas Eve an English soldier looked up as the day faded from sight. He tilted his head and motioned for silence and heard from the German lines, Silent Night.

When the Germans were done and the last notes had faded, the English voices would swell. As they joined together to return the favor and sang, The Last Noel. Various carols were traded all along the line, both sides would do their part. The singing was soft and filled with love, and came straight from the heart. When the morning sun had burned off the mist, every eye would see. Standing there on the German lines, a makeshift Christmas tree. A few Germans climbed out of their trenches, and showed that they were unarmed. The English were cautious, was this a trick, the entire line was alarmed. But a few trusting souls threw caution to the wind and climbed out to meet their foe. They walked every slowly, making their way, through the ice, the mud and the snow. Many others would join and gifts were exchanged, like plum pudding, chocolate and smokes. They shook hands and played soccer, and talked of their homes, and maybe told a few jokes. When the day was done, they returned to their lines and all of the guns were manned. They readied themselves to again go to war, in this cursed and frozen land. But on this day, a truce had been called, the bullets and shells would cease. Death turned it's back, but it would return, taking away the love and the peace. The war would last another four years, over twenty five million souls set loose. This day would be known, till the end of time, as the Christmas day truce.

Willie R. Clay

Come gather around friends and listen to me. I'll tell you about a strange fantasy. He fought for his country and shed his life's force, then flew to Valhalla on a Valkyries horse. So goes the legend of Willie R. Clay.

Alone at an outpost, one dark starless night. That's when the enemy decided to fight. Gunfire erupted and lasted till day. But the last rifle firing was Willie R. Clay's.

When we finally reached Willie we looked all around, over twenty brave enemy lay dead on the ground. We found Willie sitting all bloody and beat. He looked up and smiled, then climbed to his feet. He picked up his rifle and then walked away. So goes the legend of Willie R. Clay.

They called him a hero and home he was sent. To shake the hand of our great president. They gave him a medal and he heard the crowd roar. Then packed all his gear and went back to the war. We remember the new man they sent us that day. It was our very own Willie R. Clay.

Three times I've been shot he said with a grin. They just patch me up and send me back in. I'll die for my country, you will watch me ride by. On a Valkyries stallion, I'll ride across the sky. For a man's luck can last for just so many days. So goes the legend of Willie R. Clay.

After a battle on a dry river bed, at Willie R's foxhole they counted the dead. Inside the pit there was blood on the ground but the body of Willie just couldn't be found. Then came the thunder from high in the sky. That's when we heard Willie's fierce war cry. Hand picked by Valkyries, the choosers of the slain. The halls of Valhalla will be his domain. No one ever mentioned what happened that day. But my friend that's the legend of Willie R.

Willy . R . Clay

The Gladiator

The gladiator stood, a bloody sword by his side. He was the champion, for his opponent has died.

He has just killed a cellmate, a brother and friend. And knew that one day, his life too must end. A gladiator must fight, fight hard and win, And killing for sport, was a deadly sin. He was their puppet, to kill was their game. He had no choice, for they ruled him with chain. After each game, he went back to his cell. Until the next week, when again he'll face hell. They came to watch, to laugh and to talk. And hear the chains rattle, each time that he walked. To them he was not human, but an animal and beast. They came to see the blood, before going to the feast. Every gladiator dreams, of their one finest hour. When the blade sinks deep, and drains all their power. To die is a wish, tho they must die with pride. As they circle the arena, on their very last ride.

The Fight

The perimeter was fortified and very well protected. Charlie was in the jungle, a major attack was expected. We held the high ground, but Charlie owned the night. We knew what was coming, it would be a vicious fight. Artillery and air support was just a call away. Little did we know, bad weather would cause delay. Gordon shared my foxhole, he was my brother and friend. Later that night, he died in my arms, I never saw him again. Night brought the darkness, darkness brought the fight. All we could do was struggle to live, and pray for the morning light. Gordon got my attention, with a rigid elbow in my side. He said I can smell them coming, they are creeping up near and wide. Gunfire erupted off to our left, then suddenly all around. Charlie was charging across the front, there would soon be blood on the ground. We fought for each other, we fought to stay alive. Because of bad weather, air support would be denied.

How many charges we turned them back, I really do not recall. Only that fewer men, were left to man the wall. Out numbered and surrounded, with ammo running low. The Captain said to fix bayonets, we have no place else to go. I looked over at Gordon, he turned to look at me. He frowned and said, this is the end, and i had to agree. But we wouldn't go down without a fight, it wasn't in our blood. Charlie came at us like an angry mob, or more so, like a flood. Ammo ran out quickly, then it was bayonets, rocks, and fists. Until Charlie slowly withdrew and melted away in the mist.

The Captain called the artillery, we can't hold them again he cussed. Drop everything left, on top of this hill, we will take them to hell with us. Charlie came back in a human wave. Victory was in their sight. But the shells came down like the pouring rain, while we laid low and tight.

When the firing ceased and silence reigned, we crawled out of would be graves. At least some of us, as for the rest, they died in their man-made caves. Charlie was defeated, broken and beat. They would never try this again. And because Gordon died, in my arms, I put paper to pen.

Hurricane Irma

Half a league, half a league, half a league onward. Into the sunshine state, stormed Hurricane Irma. Forward the raging storm. From across the sea where she formed. Into the sunshine state, stormed Hurricane Irma. Forward Hurricane Irma. Was anyone dismayed. Everyone was well informed, nobody had blundered. Some chose to take a ride, others chose to not abide, and stayed behind to embrace the ride. Into the sunshine state stormed Hurricane Irma. Irma to the right of us, Irma to the left of us. Irma in front of us. Lightning and thunder. Stormed us with rain and hail. Boldly she roared and well, over beaches of sand and shell. Hitting the sunshine state with winds well over a hundred. Hit with a powerful wind, soaked down beneath the skin, floods well over the brim, charging the sunshine state, wreaking destruction. Across beaches so white, right on through the night, tornados and rising water. Reeled from the raging storm, shattered and sundered. All of us ran and hide, but not, not the first responders. Irma to the right of us, Irma to the left of us, Irma in back of us. Lightning and thunder. Stormed us with rain and hail, while house and buildings fell. The responders who had fought so well, came through the jaws of death, out of the mouth of hell. All across the sunshine state, arose the Floridians. Irma has come and went, but what destruction she rent, life will continue anew, when the sun comes shining through on the valiant Floridians.

A Baby's Unheard Cry

She might have been an astronaut. He might have been a teacher. She might have been a scientist. He might have been a preacher. She might have had a husband. He might of had a wife. But after an abortion. They did not have a life. A baby is safe, inside a womb. Until it's time to emerge. We don't have the right to terminate, murder, or to purge. The politicians that voted, to protect a woman's rights. Don't understand the baby's life, and sorrows it ignites. The baby has a right to live, granted by God above. Who are we to take away, the life, the peace, the love. The baby has a heartbeat, if you listen you can hear. When a baby's life is taken, I can't help but shed a tear. She might have been a doctor. He might have been a cook. She might have been a homemaker. He might have written books. God gave life to us all, he did this out of grace. The baby who has been aborted, will never be replaced.

A Baby's Unheard Cry

The Torch of Enlightenment

She stands high on a pedestal facing southeast.
The arriving newcomers are who she will greet.
Dressed all in green from her head to her toes,
Above her head the enlightenment torch glows.
A torch in her right hand, in her left hand a tablet.
Offering freedom and opportunity, became her habit.
Welcome to our country, come in and be free.
Abide by our laws and customs I plea.
Come here legal and don't do as you please.
And stand when you hear, "Oh say can you see."
Our flag is a symbol of our country and pride.
Many of our people, fought for it and died.
But times have changed and laws are forsaken.
Illegal immigration is plaguing our nation.
If Lady Liberty could speak to our lawmakers she'd call.
Stop all this nonsense and build the damn wall.

Darkness

I've heard that darkness does not exist, it is only the absence of light.
I myself do not believe, I don't think this is right.
Darkness comes in many forms and sometimes to extremes
It comes in depression, pain and loneliness and sometimes when we dream.
Shadows are all around us, even in the shade.
They linger close and move in nearer when light begins to fade.
Darkness lives in all of us, it doesn't make a sound.
Just stand and fight and hold your own till sunshine comes around.
Some fight the darkness everyday, and some will drink from its cup.
Just try to live and learn to fight, and never ever give up.

Love Everlasting.

Driving down the road, their bodies a foot apart. They talked and shared of many things, all coming from the heart.

He took her hand in his, and drew it slowly to his face. Kissing it soft and smooth, savouring her sweet taste.

No candle light was needed, no light from the moon above. The only light that mattered, was generated by their love.

He wrapped his arms around her, with her back against his chest. She could hear his heart beating, from the way her head was pressed.

Slow dancing in a crowded room, but feeling close and alone. The only music they could hear was the sweetness of their heart song.

Thinking Out Loud, without making a sound, their love in the same place. Heart to heart, their minds in sync, warm in their embrace.

He softly said "look at me" and she looked deep into his eyes. In them he saw, the love in her heart, he never saw any lies.

They had many conversations, but the silent ones were the best. Sometimes talking all night long, till the sun began to crest.

Whenever they were parted, they imagine the other was there. No matter what they were doing or going, they thought of the other with care.

Love can be everlasting, the strongest emotion of them all. It must be earned it must be savored and not allowed to stall.

Love EverLasting

Understanding

Why do they deal drugs to the young girls and boys,
don't they know it can lead to a bad end.
It can ruin their life, or cause them to die, don't bury
your head in the sand.
I just don't understand.
Why do some people have pets and then mistreat
them, don't they know they are family and friends.
They are neglected, starved and beaten, or released to
live off the land.
I just don't understand.
They served us with pride, but now are forgotten,
homeless and needing a helpful hand.
They have scars we can't see, and wounds that don't
bleed, all received from protecting our land.
I just don't understand.
Have you ever held a newborn, close and tight within
your love.
Don't you know that they came from heaven above.
Love and protect them from a doctor's evil hand.
I just don't understand.
Why are kids mistreated, battered and beat, don't we
know they're the future of us all.
Love them and guide them, and teach right from
wrong, teach them how to expand.
I just don't understand.
Why do we vote them into office, but they aren't
really for us, corruption and greed is the plan.
They say what we want to hear, but they don't really
care. Our vote is all they demand.

I just don't understand.
They don't want us praying to our God and creator,
they've taken him out of the schools.
When tragedy strikes, they say where was he, why
didn't he stop this with just a command.
I just don't understand.
You hear of these things, and they hurt in your heart,
you want to help, but where do you start.
Just take a step back, and then take a stand, and try to
understand.

Arlington

I served on the Arizona, I was there that infamous day.
I live a long and happy life. Before I passed away.
I do not know how I was unharmed or why I was still alive.
Only that many shipmates, are still resting deep inside.

I served in the Corps, but not very long. I died on a foreign beach.
The sun was hot, the sand was gritty, no fresh water within my reach.
But I hear we won and our flag was raised on Suribachi's volcanic ash.
I was proud to serve and died too young, I really don't want to rehash.

In the Air Force I flew a mighty warplane over the 38th parallel.
One sunny day I was caught unaware, no one would hear me yell.
My jet descended quickly, it crashed and burned upon the ground.
My remains were soon recovered, but my soul was heaven bound.

In the jungles of Nam I served as a soldier three long and terrible tours.
I survived and came home with a troubled mind, and ills that can't be cured.

I lived on the streets, I tried to forget the blood, the horror, the pain.
I died late one night, alone and forgotten, in the bitterly freezing rain.

I was a leatherneck and true to the Corps, the battle for Fallujah was my end.
We fought street by street, and house to house, me and many other men.
I was going up the stairs of a two story house, when I caught a round in my chest.
I was treated quickly but it was too late. I know the corpsman did his best.

Now we all reside together on this sacred hollowed ground.
Walk among the crosses, and try not to make a sound.
Honor us, and show respect as you quietly pass through.
Visit us as we rest in peace at 1 Memorial Avenue.

When Time Stood Still

The coach pulled down the bill of his hat to block the
glare of the lights.
He looked at the scoreboard and could plainly see,
they might not win this fight.
It was a Friday evening and the last home game, the
weather was breezy and cold.
He looked at the young man who stood by his side
and called a play that was bold.
They were down by four, with three seconds left, it
would all come down to one play.
The quarterback dropped back and threw the ball into
the skies of gray.
Then a strange thing happened, time froze still, the
ball left suspended in air.
Every player was frozen, and so was the crowd, it
was as quiet as a mouse in his lair.
The coach looked around and removed his hat, and
gazed at the young men around him.
He knew to some, he was like a father, so he tried to
guide, mold, and lead them.
He worked them hard, but he worked them fair, and
taught them to love one another.
He turned back to look into the stands and saw frozen
fathers and mothers.
He knew in his heart, they had sent him young boys
he could help to turn into men.
He gave some rides home, and lunch money to
others, he tried to be their coach and friend.
Then the clock started ticking, the noise returned, the

players were moving, the ball in the air.
The receiver was covered, and the safety was closing,
it came down to a hope and a prayer.
Six arms reached up in a tangled mess, the ball
quickly snatched from the sky.
It got deathly quiet on one side of the field, the other
side cheered in reply.
Losing is easy, it takes little effort, just learn to get up
and try again.
It is equally important to not boast and be humble,
when learning how to win.

Lambert

Lambert my pup, is like my shadow, he is with me
wherever I go.
As I write these words, he is sitting below me, licking
my foot and toe.
He knows when I am happy, he knows when I am sad.
He knows I love him with all my heart, even when I
am mad.
He loves me in my darkness, he loves me in my light.
He loves me when I scold him, for doing things that
aren't right.
We ride together in my truck, beside me he lays or
sits.
And while at work he patiently waits for time to leave
and quit.
On Monday's we stop for a special treat,
cheeseburgers are on the menu.
He gobbles them down in ten seconds flat, and hopes
this event will continue.
He goes with me on my walks, tho I wonder who is
walking who.
It's a wonder I can walk at all, cause he likes to chew
on my shoe.
A dog is called man's best friend.
He is my buddy, I am his man.

Heroes

Who runs into a burning building, to rescue children,
women and men.
Who does this knowing, they might not live to walk
back out again.
When bullets are flying and people are fleeing and
lives are being taken.
Who runs towards the gunfire knowing their own life
may soon be forsaken.
Who walks the floor in twelve hour shifts, treating the
sick and the injured.
Often spoken to harsh and sometimes mistreated, but
their care is never hindered.
Who serves our country and keeps us safe, at risk of
life and limb.
Not knowing if they will ever return, the outcome
could be quite grim.
The word hero, has no borders, it can't be defined by
color, gender, or creed.
When fear grips their heart, they push it aside, they
are a very rare breed.
Not the player who scored the winning touchdown.
During the anthem, his knee was on the ground.
Not the player who hit the winning homerun.
But won't sign a baseball, for the young.
Not the actor who stars on the silver screen.
And acts like they are kings and queens.
To be a hero you don't have to fight, you don't even
have to save a life.
Give of yourself and expect no reward, during times
of trouble and strife.

Lest We Forget

He convinced himself he was bulletproof young,
strong, and brave.
He convinced himself he would survive and return
home unscathed.
But walking point was a dangerous job so many
things to look out for.
He kept his eyes open, always alert, he was well-
trained in the Corps.
But fate has a way of changing plans, with him it was
the same.
He returned home alive but broken and beat, in a
wheelchair because he was lame.
He served his country and then was discarded
because he was no longer of use.
He was spit on and called baby killer and suffered all
kinds of abuse.
In later years agent orange took his life, how it
happened he could not recall.
All that mattered was he died in the war, but his
name is not on the wall.

Taken

He was taken from his yard, while playing near the
fence.
Who would do, such a thing, it didn't make no sense.
Picked up and roughly thrown, into the back of an
empty van.
Which then sped away, down the road, by a very
smelly man.
About an hour later, they stopped deep in the woods.
He could see through the window, this wasn't his
neighborhood.
When the door was opened, he jumped, knocking the
man to his knees.
Quickly he took off running, disappearing into the
trees.
He sat there nice and quiet, till the van had driven away.
Then slowly started walking, a long journey was
underway.
He didn't know where he was, or how far he would
need to roam.
But onward ever onward, somehow he would make it
home.
The rain started pouring down, he was hungry wet
and cold.
Somehow he knew which direction, would take him
to his abode.
For many days he traveled, avoiding people
whenever he could.
Sleeping at night, moving on, and eating things that
weren't good.

The rain continued falling, and soon turned into snow.

His feet were bruised and bloody, his head was hanging low.

And then one day he saw it, his house at the end of the road.

He saw his dad, up on the porch, his heart began to glow.

Then started running, finding energy he didn't know he had.

He couldn't wait to get there, into the loving arms of his dad.

All four legs were churning, his long ears flopping in the wind.

A long and difficult journey, he didn't want to make again.

His dad saw him coming, and slowly stood upon his feet.

The man leapt off the porch as fast as he could, to meet him in the street.

The man had found his puppy, the puppy had found his man.

Much love they felt for each other, I hope you understand.

Local Heroes

When the weather begins to deteriorate,
and the eye is very well formed.
When hurricane force winds are howling,
we can't say we were not warned.
They offer much needed services,
giving out information, supplies and more.
They risk their own safety, and do what they
can, fully knowing what could be in store.
From the firefighters and paramedics,
who will venture where others won't dare.
They rescue and provide assistance,
even after the skies have turned fair.
From the police that are out patrolling,
because looters will be out in force.
They work hard to maintain order,
till well after the storms run it's course.
From the nurses in our care centers,
who won't abandon the patients in their ward,
They continue to dispense medication,
providing comfort as they walk the floor.
From the National Guard, that will be deployed,
traveling many miles without delay.
They search and rescue and provide supplies,
to those who decided to stay.
All these professions are very much needed,
they deserve our respect and our thanks.
They are everyday people, just like us,
the women and men in the ranks.

Semper Fi

Born November 10ᵗʰ, 1775, in a dusty tavern on
Phillies east side.
Their storied service is covered with glory, blood,
honor, and pride.
You may call him leatherneck if you so wish, from the
collar that he wore.
It protected his neck from the swing of a cutlass,
Glory to the Corps.
In World War I at Belleau Wood, the French were
running in fear.
Captain Williams replied with disgust on his face.
"Retreat hell, we just got here."
Sergeant Major Daly reportedly yelled, "Come on you
sons of bitches, do you want to live forever."
Advance they did, routing the Hun, more glory and a
message to all. we will fight in any endeavor
The Germans were stopped dead in their tracks and
sent running away at a jog.
They bestowed honor and glory upon the Corps, by
calling them Devildog.
In World War II, on Iwo Jima, the most costly battle
they've been through.
The Medal Of Honor was awarded to Marines that
numbered twenty-two.
"Uncommon valor was a common virtue." Admiral
Nimitz uttered these words.
Over six thousand marines had lost their lives. Their
honor will not be deferred.
First to fight, Esprit the Corps, and Semper Fi are
words that are always seen.
Call him Gyrene, or Jarhead if you must, but when
the bullets fly, call him Marine.

Veterans Day

You can see them all around us, they are everywhere
you may go.
They work in every profession, to look at them you
would never know.
They are our nations veterans, they come from every
walk of life.
Most of them lead normal lives, while others are full
of strife.
Some of them were the tip of the spear, and saw the
horrors of war.
They never imagined when returning home, what
could be in store.
The VA tries to help them, but are under staffed and
under funded.
They medicate and isolate, leaving them feeling
useless and abandoned.
Trained to fight and sent to war, to protect us one
and all.
Then set aside when their tours were over, putting
their backs against the wall.
Some returned with visible wounds, their bodies no
longer intact.
While others return with a troubled mind, wishing
they hadn't come back.
The VA provides services to nine million vets, in
hospitals not up to par.
Each year six thousand take their own life. We must
never forget who they are.

Washington needs to understand, without these heroes where would we be.

Take care of them, like they do themselves. So the rest of the country will see.

Many have served in times of war, and many in times of peace.

Honor and thank them every day, our appreciation must never cease.

YOLO

YODA, you only die once, but maybe that's just a fable.

He looked at the three items, he had spread out on the table.

The night was pitch black, on the eve of Christmas this year.

He stared into the darkness, and cracked open an ice cold beer.

He thought about life's journey, where he'd been and what he saw.

He thought about the highs and lows, could this be the final straw.

He picked up a half empty bottle, he then took a swallow or two.

Then chased it down to his belly, with a can of near frozen brew.

He snuck a peek at the loaded gun, placed carefully out of his reach.

Thinking about that terrible day, when he fought on that bloody beach.

Life had not been kind, but at least he was still in one piece.

He thought about the horrible dreams, on nights that seemed not to cease.

The more he drank the more he saw, in the clouds of confusion in his head.

The taste of the smoke, the smell of the blood, the bodies of so many dead.

Then all at once, he cocked his head, in the darkness he began to hear.

Christmas carolers singing a song, spreading some Christmas cheer.

Then he stood up, slowly shaking his head, and reached for the weapon of doom.

And walked away, down the short hall, and put it away in his room.

YOLO, you only live once, maybe that too is just a fable.

He had thought of a baby, born in the night, in a very small stable.

Angel of Mercy

She slowly climbed into her car, bone weary with heavy eyes.
A cup of coffee in her hand, just trying to energize.
She was an angel of mercy, a nurse, caregiver and more,
Three months ago she didn't know what tragedy was in store.
A deadly killer from across the sea, would assault us with such force.
Nothing to do but isolate, and let it run its course.
For doctors and nurses all over the land, from sea to shining sea.
Working overtime and risking it all, helping you and me.
Wearing her scrubs and wearing a mask, and breathing her own hot air.
She has a family she loves very much so removing it she didn't dare.
A double shift was often required with so many sick and in bed.
She wanted to stop and close her eyes and clear her sleepy head.
But on she went to do what she could on feet that were tired and sore.
Every day she logged many miles, on her ward just walking the floor.
Show them respect whenever you can, as they work with a loving heart.
They are on the front lines, fighting this battle, just trying to do their part.

The Corpsman

A navy corpsman, an honorary marine. His brothers
he did embrace.
He'd never been to Parris Island, but had camo on his
young face.
He knew each of them by name, and listened to their
stories of home.
Learned of their families and sweethearts, and places
they would love to roam.
He tended to their every wound, and drained their
blistered feet.
Praying the medical supplies would last, and would
not soon depleat.
In a fire fight, skirmish, or battle, he was always on
the front line.
He knew the screams of incoming mortars, and the
sound of a bullet whine.
While the brave marines were returning fire, and
keeping their heads low.
He looked around and listened close, when he heard
"corpsman up" he'd go.
Nevermind the gunfire, nevermind the smoke,
nevermind the sand and rock.
Plugging wounds, a tourniquet or two, and treating
those who were in shock.
He heard grown men cry for their mothers, told them
they would be fine.
He hid his tears and held their hands, not caring if lies
crossed the line.

Then one day while tending a brother, a bullet was fired, drilling him real clean.
He died a hero, but not alone, he died a brother marine.
Honor the corpman,honor the medic, and the nurses and doctors in the rear.
They fight to treat our wounded warriors, they do this dispite their fear.

The Honorable Elder

The old man sat in his rocking chair and ran his hands through his thin gray hair. He looked at the flag that hung on the post and stared at it like it was a ghost.

It reminded him of the youth he had spent, in the snows of Korea where he had been sent. He had fought with Chesty at what is called Frozen Chosen, every man returned home, the wounded, the living and the frozen.

The white strips reminded him of the snow and the ice. That frozen ground was no paradise. The red represented the blood that was shed, and the countless men who ended up dead.

The blue field resembled the sadness he felt, from the horrors of war in his heart where it dwelt. Fifty white stars one for each state. He could remember when there was forty-eight.

From the sands of Parris Island to the South Korean shore. From the war-torn battlefield to his front door. From a young, scared kid, who was only twenty. To a combat veteran who had seen plenty.

Now he sits in his chair with a tear in his eye, and watched the flag, trying to understand why. At home in these days the flag was rejected. It was spit on and burned and was not respected.

He sips his beer and slowly shakes his gray head. And wonders if today's youth would dare. He had fought for her once when he had been called. He would do it again, even if he had to crawl.

I See

I see said the blind man, I see things you can't
possibly imagine.
I see with my ears, I see with my hands, I see with my
nose and emotion
I see the sunshine, by the warmth on my skin. I see
moisture in the air, as a new day begins.
I see smiles and laughter, on the face of the child. I see
the fragrance on flowers, that grow in the wild.
I see birds flying, by the beat of their wings. I see
crystal clear water, when I drink from a spring.
I see the sorrow, when somebody dies. I see the
loneliness, when a whippoorwill cries.
I see the love, from a four-legged friend. I see new
life, on the breath of the wind.
I see the silence, in the still of the night. I see the
turmoil, on those who will fight.
I see the sweat, on a hard-working man. I see the
tenderness, in an exhausted woman.
I see the sadness, every time a tear drops. I see
branches swaying, up in the treetops.
I see salt in the air, at the shore of the ocean. I see
hearts floating by, when love is in motion.
I see said the blind man. Close your eyes and you will
too. Open your mind and your heart, and see as I do.

Live and Let Live

Why would you hate a man, for the color of his skin. Do you know his life story. Do you know where he's been. Did you know he feels pain, on his body, and in his heart. Do you know he feels sadness when he and loved ones are apart. Did you know when he is hurt, his blood is just as red. Have you ever listened to his heart, or the words that he has said. Is it a man's choice, to be yellow, brown, black, or white. Why hate a man for the way he looks, somehow this ain't right. We are all made by the Creator, the color is his choice, if you think back to the beginning we are all brothers, so rejoice.

Why would you hate a person, because they are lesbian or gay. Do you take the time to learn their heart, or do you look away. Did you know they all have families, they love with all their heart. Maybe if you try to understand, you would know just where to start. Begin with what is beating deep inside their chest. Or the way they think, and how they love, and how they give their best. They may live close, just down the road. Take time to know their soul. Think of their heart, think of their love, think of their life's role. We are all made by the Creator who are we to judge. Love them all, as does our God, who doesn't hold a grudge.

Why would you hate a person, for the religion that

they chose. Did you know God loves all of us, from
our head down to our toes. Do you know about their
customs, does God turn a blind eye. Did you know
we will stand before him, the instant that we die.
The Bible tells many stories, that can be interpreted
in many ways. How do you know the thoughts of
God, or his words on Judgment Day. Wars have
been fought, since the beginning of time. All because
your form of worship, is different than mine. We are
all made by the Creator, the story is available to all.
Learn to accept the beliefs of others, or we will see
mankind fall.

The Wall

From Buis, to Vandergeer, and so very many in
between.
Includes the names of Sailors, Soldiers, Airmen, and
Marines.
It stretches over 246 feet, from the East to the West.
Most were young, some were older, but all gave their
best.
More are added every year, on Mother's Day their
names inscribed. The pain their death caused their
loved ones can never be described.
I once saw a man walking along the wall, head and
eyes down low.
He didn't look at the panels, he knew where he
wanted to go.
He stopped at one of the panels, and touched two
names with his hand.
I don't know what he was thinking, maybe the pain,
the jungle, or the sand.
He slowly dropped down to his knees, like kneeling
before a cross. And placed a book in front of him,
maybe thinking about his loss.
He then lit a cigarette, and then quietly lit another.
Placing them on either side, one for each of his
brothers.
Looking up at the names, he slowly placed another
one between his lips. Maybe thinking about his
friends and how they died in that horrible conflict.
I didn't intrude, I stayed well away, I let him have his

space. I just sat down and watch this sadness, with tears running down my face.

Our veterans have their special day, we honor them in November.

Our fallen warriors gave all of their days, please let them be remembered.

D Day

Can you imagine stepping off a landing craft, young
and full of life. Unaware if your next step, will make a
widow of your wife.
Or maybe being so young, not even old enough to
vote. But stepping forward, scared to death, your
heart caught in your throat.
Onward you move through the water, then onward
onto the sand. Fighting to give freedom, to those who
love this land.
Bullets whiz around you, shells exploding all-around.
You want to stop and dig a hole, deep into the ground.
But forward you keep moving, past brothers and a
few friends. Moving towards the sea wall, through
the carnage that does not end.
You make it to your appointed spot, your body
without a scratch. The fear you feel runs deep inside,
nothing will ever match.
The lieutenant is dead, the sergeant is missing, few
faces you recognize. All you see is other soldiers, with
the same fear in their eyes.
Returning fire you do your best to keep the enemy's
head low. Allowing more men to reach the wall,
without suffering a fatal blow.
Slowly but surely more men arrived to keep the
Germans at bay. The sun is hot and water is scarce,
this is the longest day.
Remember the men who made it, remember the
fallen as well. Remember those who keep us safe,
while walking their personal hell.

My Flag

My flag, stained in red, from the blood of Soldiers,
Airman, Sailors, and Marines.
From Bunker Hill to the deserts of Afghanistan.
And every battle and war in between.

Many have fought, many have died. Just to help keep
our country free.
Fighting for us, for our way of life, they fought for
"Oh say can you see."
They died in the air, the jungles and mountains, they
died upon the sea.
Giving their lives, their very last breath, never asking
" what's in it for me"

My flag, stained in blue. From the sadness and sorrow
it brings.
Mothers and fathers, who lost their young. Both men
and women it seems.
The children who cry, when mom can't come home,
and dads who can't hug them again.
The pain and the hurt, they will carry through life, I
just don't know where to begin.

The husbands and wives, that lost their spouses, and
finding love no more.
The military car, that pulls in their drive, the dreaded
knock on the door.
My flag, stained in white. From the youths, who's
lives has been spent.

They didn't want to die in a war, or return with
bodies broken and bent.

The Innocence lost, when the first shot is fired, the
horrors they feel in their heart.
The fear they have, they still man the line, knowing
their soul may soon part.
21 guns and a folded flag, won't replace the lives that
have perished.
Pictures and memories are all that remains, these
things will always be cherished.

Our banner, our flag, will lead us
on, it will get us through the storm.
We are now living in troubled times, the riots and
destruction must end.
How will we learn, to live in peace, when evil won't
let it begin.
Our symbol of freedom it is spit on and burned, and
treated like a rag.
Our symbol of freedom is much more than that, my
Country, my Nation, my Flag.
...

My Flag

A Light Within the Darkness.

A soldier lay on the battlefield, with wounds that promised a dead man. Blood flowed slowly upon the ground like small rivers into the sand.

The Angel came from the starry Heavens, on silver wings as silent as the night. Her long blond hair flowing like a cloud, a brilliant halo providing the light.

Through the smoky night she glided, landing gently beside where he rest. She lifted his upper body, and pulled him tightly to her breasts.

Whispering words of comfort, tho unconscious he heard every word she spew. Stay strong if you want to see the sunrise. Future generations are counting on you.

Then the soldier felt strong hands, son, it's me, your father. I know what you can do. Use the strength, that is in your heart, and know I am so proud of you.

Next he felt a tender touch, that reached down into his soul. My son don't let a mother grieve, I love you, fight and be whole.

His sweetheart kissed him softly, upon lips that were parched and dry. Baby, I need and love you, please don't make me tell you goodbye.

The Angel continued holding the soldier, there was not much else she could do. Tears were forming in her eyes, my child this is all up to you.

In the distance she heard the chopper, the Medics would be here soon. Wiping the tears with a lock from her hair, her heart beginning to swoon.

The soldier would live, it wasn't his time, but he had to do his part. Slowly she lifted and floated away, knowing the strength had come from his heart.

Life Precious Life

Gunfire erupts all night and all day, on streets that are nasty and gritty. You might think this is Mogadishu, Fallujah, Baghdad, or Hue City.

Businesses are looted, buildings are burned, our monuments defaced and destroyed. The innocent people trapped inside, not safe, very hungry and unemployed.

Black lives matter, with that I agree, but all other lives matter too. Black, white, brown, and yellow and even the ones who wear blue.

When attacked or threatened you called 911, expecting help of some kind. But police are defunded and risking it all, Injustice no longer is blind.

The deaths that hurt the worst in my heart, the deaths that cause the most pain. Our precious young flowers, our babies and youth, I just don't know how to explain.

A beautiful little girl, a handsome young boy, their lives ended without cause. Much too young to know or understand, still believing in Old Santa Claus.

When life begins, I don't really know, but I believe it's early in the womb. Their lives are ended before they breathe air, little flowers not allowed to bloom.

The destruction and violence must end, and end soon. The killing of kids must stop. So we as a nation can recover and heal, before we bleed out drop by drop.

The Thin Blue Line

He kissed them on their foreheads, as they lay
sleeping in their beds. Three special little flowers, as
he watched them a tear he shed.

His shift was starting shortly, a long one would be
in the cards. The Thin Blue Line was still intact they
were still the city's guards.

But events were unfolding, events you never would
have guessed. He walked out the door, his love by his
side, his uniform perfectly pressed.

She kissed him softly on the lips, and pleaded be safe,
and come back home. Each day she worried, and
dreaded hearing, the ringing of the phone.

Black Lives Matter was rioting again, just like
so many days before. There was talk of police
defunding, across the country from shore to shore.

The day had gone by quickly, the sun soon dropping
out of sight. The city was in turmoil. buildings of fire
would engulf the night.

Later that night his wife put the kids to bed, then sat
down and waited, in his favorite chair. Her nerves
were stressed her palms were sweaty, she wished that
he was there.

She thought about his gentle touch, and his handsome and warm dark face. She thought how it felt to be in his arms, in his powerful strong embrace.

But never again would he open the door, no longer would he breathe air. He was shot and killed while doing his duty, he would never again stroke her hair.

A few cops are bad, but most are good, in every profession this is true. They are out there defending, upholding the law, support the line of blue.

Tears of the Veteran

A shot rings out in the midnight air, a veteran has ended his life. Do we know what he was suffering from? Do we know his pain or his strife?

He drank to silence the demons in his head, or at least to cloud the fears. When he could afford it, a bottle of cheap whiskey, he drank it mixed with his tears.

The battles fought, the lives that were taken. While in a warrior state. He felt very old in his heart and soul, this young soldier of only twenty-eight.

Battle scars both inside and out. The internal one hurt the most. By day he fought the demons in his head, and at night he fought the ghosts.

He told his stories as painful as it was, of death in the deserts and hills. Seeking help from a few Vets centers, all they could offer him was pills.

He knew his God was all forgiving, but how could he be saved by grace? He rarely looked into a mirror, he couldn't stand to see his own face.

It Happened One Night when the moon was high, he couldn't take it anymore. Death seemed better than living like this, he needed to escape a war.

Full military honors were bestowed on this hero, scores of medals upon his chest. Buried at Arlington with many brothers, his mind was finally at rest.

Call him weak, call him a quitter, condemn his soul to hell if you must. When his country called, and bullets were flying, he was definitely a man you could trust.

A shot rings out in the midnight air, another veteran has ended his life. Do we know what he was suffering from? Do we know of his pain or his strife?

Both men and women join the service, they willingly answer our country's call. Some need help and never receive it, and by their own hand they fall.

CPSIA information can be obtained
at www.ICGtesting.com
Printed in the USA
BVHW031519150421
605031BV00009B/790